THE OFFICIAL
HEART OF MIDLOTHIAN
ANNUAL 2022

Written by Sven Houston
Designed by Daniel Brawn

CONTENTS

CAPTAIN'S
WELCOME

Hello and welcome to the Heart of Midlothian Football Club Annual 2022.

Within the pages of this year's annual, you can read all about what was a very strange 2020/21 season for both players and supporters.

The effects of the COVID-19 pandemic were well and truly felt as we were left with no choice but to play an entire season without you, our supporters. I can't tell you how strange it was to play competitive games at Tynecastle without the maroon faithful in the stands and I sincerely hope we never have to experience that again.

We obviously went into the season having been demoted from the Premiership once the 19/20 season was curtailed due to the pandemic. The injustice we felt about that decision motivated us throughout the season in the Championship and we were delighted to go on and clinch 1st place and an immediate return to the top-flight of Scottish football.

For me personally, it was a privilege to return to the club I supported as a boy. I always had it in my head that I wanted to return to Hearts one day and when the opportunity presented itself, I grabbed it with both hands. This season I've also had the added honour of being named Club Captain (for a second time!) and I can't explain how much this means to me.

Running out on to the Tynecastle turf with the armband on, hearing the roar of the Gorgie crowd; it's something truly special and I will never, ever take it for granted.

Hearts, Hearts, Glorious Hearts!

Craig Gordon
Captain

2020/21

A SEASON LIKE NO OTHER

As Hearts entered 2020, much of the focus was on the January transfer window as then manager Daniel Stendel looked to reshape the squad ahead of a huge second half to the season. No one could have quite envisaged how the season would pan out, however, as the Covid-19 pandemic brought the world to a standstill. The league season was curtailed in March and Hearts, bottom of the league at the time, were demoted to the Championship. Despite a long legal battle, the decision could not be overturned and the Jambos - now led by Robbie Neilson - set about preparing for a season like no other

2020/21

Having been forced to wait until October for the Championship season to commence, the boys in maroon came flying out the traps as they trounced Dundee 6-2 in the opening game in front of 20,000 empty seats at Tynecastle. The reality of a season behind closed doors well and truly set in, as what should have been a memorable night under the lights in front of a full house turned out to be rather surreal given the circumstances.

Neilson's men followed up with a 1-0 victory away to Arbroath the following week, before Hampden came calling as the Scottish Cup semi-finals from the previous season finally came round. The opponents? Hibs. Despite having only had a handful of competitive games (in contrast to our city rivals, who kicked off the season months earlier), the Jambos once again reigned supreme at the national stadium. Goals from Craig Wighton and Liam Boyce sealed a 2-1 win over the Leith side to book a place in the final against Celtic.

OCTOBER

The month of November began with a 2-1 league win over Inverness CT at Tynecastle before East Fife were defeated 3-2 in the final Betfred Cup Group stage game.

The first defeat of the season then came at East End Park as a sub-par performance saw Dunfermline win 2-1 under the lights in Fife.

The Jambos responded with a 3-0 home win over Alloa four days later, however, that very same opponent then caused a Betfred Cup upset as a late penalty earned them a 1-0 victory at the Indodrill - thereby eliminating Hearts out at the first knock-out stage.

Hearts kicked off the countdown to Christmas with a 2-0 win against Morton at Cappielow before obliterating Queen of the South at Tynecastle in a 6-1 victory. It was the perfect preparation for the Scottish Cup Final.

Celtic took a 2-0 lead into half-time at Hampden, only for Liam Boyce and Stephen Kingsley to haul the Jambos level in the second half. Into extra-time, Leigh Griffiths made it 3-2 before Josh Ginnelly levelled again. It was to end in heart break, however, as Celtic won the match on penalties.

Hearts responded with a 5-3 win over Ayr United at Tynecastle on Boxing Day before beating Arbroath 3-1 three days later.

DECEMBER

JANUARY

It was a miserly start to 2021 as Dundee won 3-1 at Dens Park on January 2nd. Two weeks later, Alloa were beaten 3-1 at the Indodrill before Raith Rovers snatched a 3-2 win at Tynecastle. Revenge was sweet, however, as the boys in maroon won 4-0 in Kirkcaldy just a few days later.

The month ended with a solid 1-0 win over Dunfermline at Tynecastle.

Into February and a slump in form. A 1-0 win away to Ayr United was followed by a 1-1 draw at Queen of the South and then draws with Greenock Morton and Inverness CT respectively.

FEBRUARY

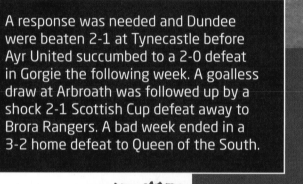

A response was needed and Dundee were beaten 2-1 at Tynecastle before Ayr United succumbed to a 2-0 defeat in Gorgie the following week. A goalless draw at Arbroath was followed up by a shock 2-1 Scottish Cup defeat away to Brora Rangers. A bad week ended in a 3-2 home defeat to Queen of the South.

MARCH

SCOTTISH
CHAMPIONSHIP

WINNERS 2020/21
HEART OF MIDLOTHIAN F.C.

Into the final month of the season with the Championship title all but secured. A 0-0 draw at Dunfermline was followed up with a 6-0 home win against Alloa. Another goalless draw at Morton was played out before the Jambos lifted the title in a 3-0 home win against Inverness CT. The season was then wrapped up with an impressive 4-0 victory at Raith.

APRIL

A SEASON OF EMPTY STANDS

The 20/21 season saw football supporters locked out of grounds across the country and around the globe as the COVID-19 pandemic put a hold on life as we know it.

Club photographer David Mollison was among the few who still got to take in every Hearts game in the Championship winning season. His images show life behind closed doors in Scottish football.

he Hearts team make their way from their temporary essing room down through the empty terraces and nto the pitch for a clash with Ayr United on a cold ebruary night in 2021. A Liam Boyce penalty sealed 1-0 win for the boys in maroon.

Nothing but empty stands as Andy Halliday delivers a ball into the box at East End Park on November 20th. Dunfermline inflicted a 2-1 defeat on Robbie Neilson's side that night.

Is there anyone out there?

Steven Naismith and Andy Halliday flank Liam Boyce who has just fired home the winner against Hibs in the Scottish Cup Semi Final on October 31st 2020.

Captain Steven Naismith hoists the Championship trophy at Tynecastle on the final home game of the season as journalists watch on from the Main Stand press zone.

Liam Boyce converts a penalty in front of cardboard supporters on the opening day of the 20/21 season. The Jambos kicked off life in the second tier with an emphatic 6-2 win over Dundee at Tynecastle.

A goalless draw away to Arbroath in March 2021 didn't stop David Mollison from capturing this striking image of an aerial duel in the home box as Armand Gnanduillet and Liam Boyce go for the ball.

Hampden heartbreak for the Jambos as Celtic claim a penalty shootout victory five days before Christmas 2020.

Marius Žaliukas

FOREVER IN OUR HEARTS

26

From the boardroom to the stands, everyone connected with the Heart of Midlothian Football Club was shocked and saddened to learn that Marius Žaliukas had passed away in October 2020 after a brave struggle against motor neurone disease.

During his time in the capital, this engaging young man was a fine player, extremely popular with his teammates and a great favourite with the supporters. Accordingly, he will long be remembered at Tynecastle Park.

Marius was born on November 10th 1983 in Kaunas, Lithuania, and with physical presence and positional skills, he was an outstanding central defender who became Hearts' captain in August 2010. In addition, the towering Lithuanian was a regular International player, gaining 25 caps for his homeland between 2006 and 2016.

Marius came to Edinburgh in August 2006, initially on loan from Kaunas FBK, where he twice won the Lithuanian League Championship (2004 and 2006) and was twice on the winning side in the Lithuanian Cup Final (2004 and 2005). He played regularly in European competitions and the 6'2" defender also had previous experience with two other clubs in Lithuania: FK Inkaras Kaunas and FK Šilute.

Marius played a big part in Hearts claiming third place in the SPL in 2008-09 and fully merited his

MARIUS
ŽALIUKAS
1983 - 2020

CAPTAIN.
LEADER.
LEGEND.

18-month loan extension, despite being sent-off four times. Marius was, in fact, appointed vice-captain for 2009-10, although he was badly missed during the first half of that season, due to ankle and hamstring injuries.

Manager Jim Jefferies, promoted the big stopper to captain the following season and when his contract with Kaunas FBK expired, Marius was signed on a permanent basis, from November 2010 until the summer of 2013. He led Hearts to third place in the SPL in 2010/11 and, of course, Marius famously captained Hearts to a 5-1 victory over Hibernian in the Scottish Cup Final of 2012.

Due to injury and suspension, he was sorely missed in the League Cup Final against St. Mirren in March 2013, and then sadly, Marius left the club in the summer of 2013 after Hearts went into administration.

After trial periods with both Rangers and Queens Park Rangers, Marius signed for Championship club Leeds United, in October 2013. He then moved to Rangers in July 2014 and played against Hearts in the Championship Division before moving back home to Lithuania in August 2015. Marius subsequently played for Žalgiris Vilnius.

The majestic Lithuanian defender has made more appearances for Hearts than any other overseas player, with 222 competitive games and 15 goals. His beaming smile when holding the Scottish Cup in 2012 is an iconic moment in Hearts' history. Marius also has legendary status in Lithuania, where he is regarded as an inspiration to young players who want to appear in the top leagues of Europe.

SCOTTISH CUP
2012
WINNERS

1891   1896
1901   1906
1956   1998
2006   2012

HEART OF
MIDLOTHIAN
FOOTBALL CLUB

2021/22
FIRST TEAM SQUAD

1
CRAIG GORDON
Goalkeeper

2
MICHAEL SMITH
Defender

3
STEPHEN KINGSLEY
Defender

4 JOHN SOUTTAR
Defender

5 PETER HARING
Midfielder

6 BENI BANINGIME
Midfielder

7 JAMIE WALKER
Midfielder

8 AARON MCENEFF

Midfielder

9 BEN WOODBURN

Striker

10 LIAM BOYCE

Striker

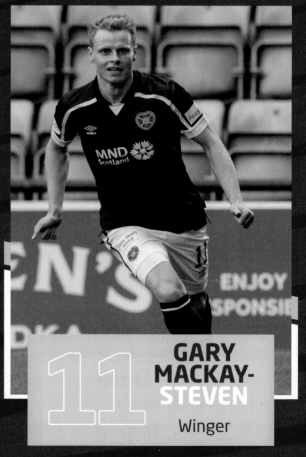

11 GARY MACKAY-STEVEN

Winger

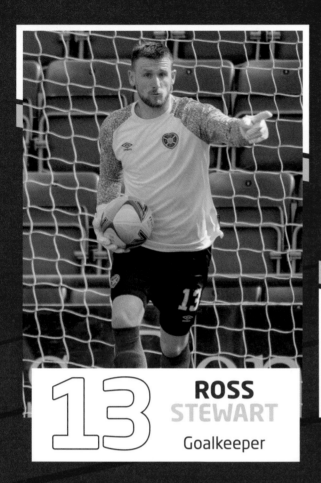

13 ROSS STEWART
Goalkeeper

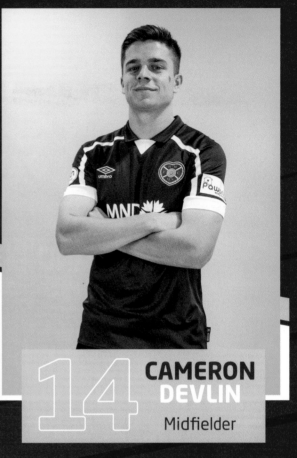

14 CAMERON DEVLIN
Midfielder

15 TAYLOR MOORE
Defender

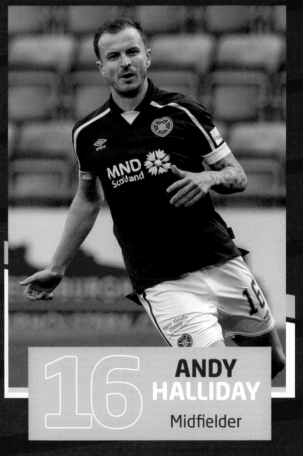

16 ANDY HALLIDAY
Midfielder

17

ALEX
COCHRANE

Defender

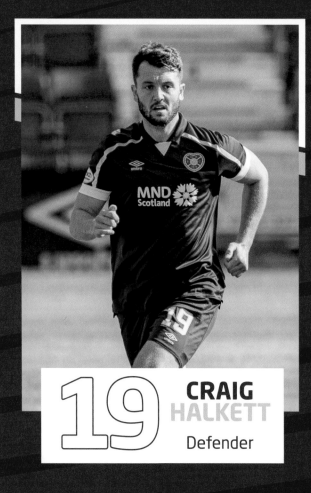

19

CRAIG
HALKETT

Defender

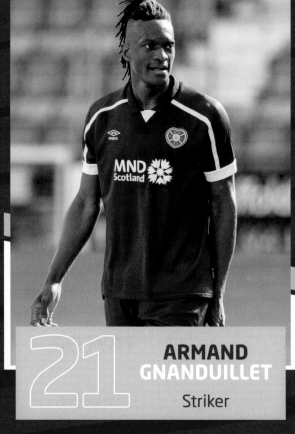

21

ARMAND
GNANDUILLET

Striker

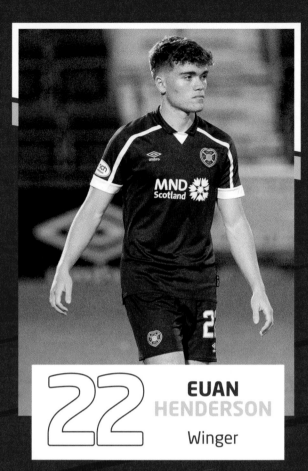

22
EUAN HENDERSON
Winger

27
CONNOR SMITH
Winger

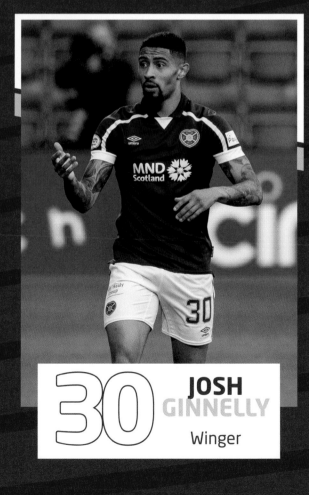

30
JOSH GINNELLY
Winger

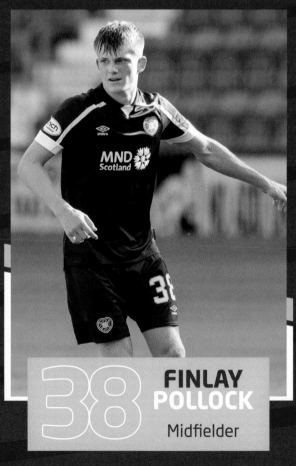

38
FINLAY POLLOCK
Midfielder

WORD SEARCH

Can you find the Hearts related words in the below wordsearch? Give it your best shot!

L	H	W	N	T	K	J	K	K	D	F	N
G	D	X	Z	K	L	A	E	M	X	Y	O
R	O	X	X	N	W	M	L	B	M	Z	S
G	O	R	G	I	E	B	T	L	X	K	T
J	T	H	D	E	L	O	S	S	G	K	R
N	K	H	C	O	S	S	A	F	M	R	E
L	O	Y	B	K	N	K	C	N	R	L	B
R	O	O	A	R	U	M	E	L	N	V	O
B	L	C	R	I	L	N	N	L	N	V	R
C	E	V	L	A	F	R	Y	Y	G	F	L
L	P	A	Y	C	M	W	T	Q	B	Y	M
R	Z	L	E	K	C	O	L	L	R	D	P

Boyce   Jambos   Skacel

Gordon   Locke   Tynecastle

Gorgie   Maroon   Zaliukas

Robertson

Answers on Page 60-61

2Red

SPOT THE BALL

Can you spot the correct ball position in this photo from when Hearts took on Inverness?

Answers on Page 60-61

WHO AM I?

Can you guess which former Hearts player I am based on the clues below?

1. I was signed by Craig Levein.

2. One of my former clubs is Hibs.

3. I won the Scottish Cup with Hearts.

4. I left Hearts in 2007.

5. I have been the manager of Dundee.

Answers on Page 60-61

FORMER PLAYER QUIZ

How many former Hearts players can you name based on the questions below?

1. I scored two goals in the famous 4-0 win over Celtic in 2017. Who am I?

2. I'm a defender who signed from Arbroath in 2001 and have had two spells at the club, re-signing in 2011. Who am I?

3. I scored four goals in my debut in a 5-1 win against Hibs in 2002. Who am I?

4. I am the club's record appearance holder. Who am I?

5. I am a goal machine who won the Scottish Cup with Hearts in 2006 and 2012. Who am I?

6. I played alongside Dave McPherson in central defence in the 1998 Scottish Cup Final. Who am I?

7. I've played for the club as a central defender and I've also been Hearts Manager on two occasions. Who am I?

8. I'm a left back who joined the club in 2005 having won the European Championship with Greece the year before. Who am I?

9. I scored the injury time equaliser in a 4-4 draw with Hibs at Tynecastle. Who am I?

10. I scored Hearts' second goal in the famous 4-0 win over Celtic in 2017. Who am I?

| 1. |
| 2. |
| 3. |
| 4. |
| 5. |
| 6. |
| 7. |
| 8. |
| 9. |
| 10. |

Answers on Page 60-61

HEARTS WOMEN

FIRST YEAR AT THE TOP

It was a big year for Hearts Women as they completed their first season playing in SWPL1, which is the highest level of women's football in Scotland.

Although the team had a very difficult season and didn't manage many wins, they made huge improvements through the season and the managers at both Rangers and Celtic were very complimentary of the positive changes made to the team over the year.

The highlights of the season included a fantastic 1-0 victory over Hibernian in December 2020 with a 90th minute goal by Paige McAllister winning the match, and an excellent 2-1 victory away to Forfar Farmington when a Lia Tweedie header and a Monica Forsyth top-corner shot from the edge of the box earned three points towards the end of the season.

There was also some great news when goalkeeper Charlotte Parker-Smith was named in the Scottish Women's Football Team of the Year. Although Hearts had lost many games, Charlotte prevented those games from being much worse, and her saves also helped to gain points where they may have been lost.

Charlotte also won the Scottish Women's Football Save of the Season award, for a flying save to stop Priscila Chinchilla, a Glasgow City player, from scoring against her in May 2021. The save was so impressive that even Craig Gordon helped Charlotte gather votes for the award on social media, and when Charlotte won the award, Craig was there to present her with the trophy after visiting the women's team at training one evening.

Promising signs indeed for the Jambo Girls, and the future is very bright for all of them.

TYNECASTLE
THROUGH
THE YEARS

Tynecastle Park has been the home of the Heart of Midlothian Football Club for a remarkable period of 135 years. While this is not the longest term of occupancy among Britain's major football clubs (Preston North End have been at Deepdale since 1875), it ranks among the top ten, and over the intervening years, our venerable ground has witnessed almost all the significant changes that have made football the most exciting game in the world, both to play and watch.

1945

Tynecastle from the air

Over the next few pages we dive into the Tynecastle image vaults for a look at how our famous ground has evolved over the decades.

A bumper crowd at the Gorgie Road end

1955

19

1962

Tynecastle from above

From the air

Celebrating a Hearts goal

83

1991

1991

The Shed

Construction of the new Main Stand

2017

2017 **2018**

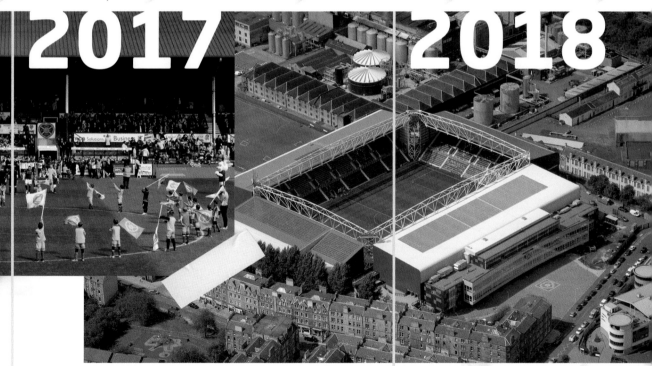

The final game in front of the Old Main Stand

Modern day Tynecastle

THE HEARTS ARRIVE IN GORGIE

By David Speed

Since the club was formed in 1874, Hearts had played at the East Meadows, then Powburn, and finally Powderhall. It was important to settle down and establish an identity, and in February 1881, the Committee made the astute decision to lease a field at Tynecastle, in the developing industrial suburb of Dalry. Hearts' influential captain, Tom Purdie, already worked in that district at the North British Rubber Mill in Fountainbridge, and so did the wife of Hearts' first goalkeeper and founder-member, Jake Reid. Over the years, many players and officials would be employed at this vast complex which became a hotbed of Hearts supporters.

On February 19th 1881, Hearts' first match at Tynecastle Park ended in a 2-1 defeat against local rivals, St.Bernards, before a healthy crowd of 1,000. However, the ground was officially opened on April 9th 1881 against another city club, Hanover, and this time, Hearts won by a handsome score of 8-0.

GRAND FOOTBALL MATCHES.

OPENING OF TYNECASTLE PARK.

HANOVER V. HEART OF MID-LOTHIAN.
AND
LANCEFIELD V. 2D HEART OF MID-LOTHIAN.
TO-DAY (SATURDAY), 9TH APRIL.
Kick-Off at 4 P.M.

ADMISSION 6d. Ladies Free.

The club subsequently flourished at Tynecastle and became established as one of the leading teams in Scotland.

At that time, Gorgie - with its enormous glue factory, grain mills and leather works - lay slightly further west, but it rapidly expanded to absorb the area of Tynecastle. The focal point of the district was the Tynecastle Toll Gate which stood on the site of what became the Tivoli Cinema. In previous years, this was where a fee was paid to use the road into central Edinburgh.

The club's new home was not the present ground, but a substantial field with space for two football pitches that ran north-south on the site of what is presently Wardlaw Street and Wardlaw Place. The nearest buildings were Morrison's Cabinet Works and the houses of White Park, both situated on the ground's eastern boundary, and the Caledonian Railway on its south side. Having two pitches allowed Hearts to regularly play two matches as an attraction to the public.

It was several months before Tynecastle Park could boast a Pavilion for the players' privacy and, for a short period, they had to wash and dress at a public house, which was then known as the Midlothian Arms (now known as the Tynecastle Arms). By 1883, a grandstand had been erected in front of the Pavilion. This wooden structure held around 250 spectators and the players entered the field through a tunnel in the Stand. Progress was evident, but games were often spoiled by the pronounced slope that ran down the pitch from the railway end to Mid-Calder Road (now Gorgie Road).

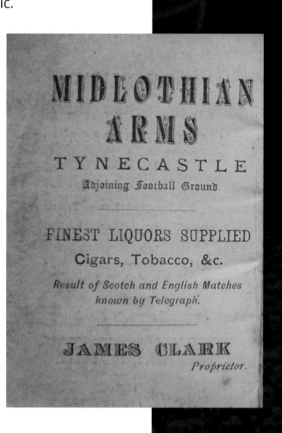

MIDLOTHIAN ARMS

TYNECASTLE

Adjoining Football Ground

FINEST LIQUORS SUPPLIED

Cigars, Tobacco, &c.

Result of Scotch and English Matches known by Telegraph.

JAMES CLARK

Proprietor.

Many spectators arrived on horse-drawn cabs, in which five fares from the Tron Kirk cost 5/- (25 pence).

These cabs made an impressive sight as they lined-up on Gorgie Road waiting for return fares, and their roofs also offered many youngsters their first view of the Hearts. The Edinburgh Tramway Company quickly realized that Hearts' games provided lucrative business and on match days, additional horse-drawn cars rumbled out to the terminus at Ardmillan Terrace. Routes could be further developed after the city limits were extended in 1882 to incorporate Tynecastle.

On April 8th 1882, Aston Villa became the first English team to play in Edinburgh and they defeated Hearts at Tynecastle by a comfortable margin of 6-2. There was no such trouble in an Edinburgh FA Cup-tie on September 30th 1882 when the team recorded its biggest victory at the ground, Holyrood being demolished by 20-2.

Hearts' only trophy success during their five-year occupancy of the first Tynecastle Park was winning the initial Rosebery Charity Cup competition on April 21st 1883. Nevertheless, the club had built up a solid fan base with between 3,000 and 5,000 watching important fixtures. The largest crowd to watch the "maroons" play across the street was 6,500. This was the attendance on October 20th 1883, when Hibs won 4-1 in the Scottish FA Cup. The ground record was established on February 25th 1882, when a reported attendance of nearly 8,000 watched the Edinburgh FA Cup Final between Hibernian and St. Bernards.

The last match on the old ground took place on 27 February 1886, with Hearts beating Sunderland by 2-1.

Because a long lease was not available, the first Tynecastle had never been fully developed and, in addition, the sloping pitch caused lengthy stoppages as the ball had to be regularly retrieved from the main road. Accordingly, the Committee decided that the club should move, but only one hundred yards, because the ever-expanding district of Gorgie-Dalry was a perfect home for Hearts.

At one time, the area's arable and livestock farms supplied the city, but this changed in the middle of the 1800s, due to the influence of the Caledonian Railway, whose main line is today the West Approach Road. t also had branch lines to Haymarket, Haymarket West and Granton, while extensive sheds were built at Dalry Road. The Haymarket Branch, opened in 1853, still carries traffic over Gorgie Road. Good communications attracted large developments, including Dalry Cemetery and

the Magdalene Asylum and Reformatory. Industries also appeared with a builder's yard at Tynecastle Toll, a coal depot, a laundry, an iron works, and a cabinet maker's factory.

When Hearts arrived in 1881, the area had further expanded with tenements extending as far as White Park. Growth was relentless and thousands more came into the district to work in world-famous companies, ncluding the Caledonian Distillery, Jeffrey's Brewery, the North British Rubber Mill, McEwan's Brewery, McVitie & Price, and our good neighbours of long standing, the North British Distillery. There was also an extensive piggery in Dalry Meadows where the school would eventually be built.

Hearts' final move commenced on Saturday, July 18th 1885, when the Edinburgh Evening News reported a special meeting of club members. James Pretsell, who was hugely influential in the field of education and would soon become President of Hearts, reported that the club had been offered an eight-year lease of Councilor James Steel's park, just across the road from the present ground. A motion that the club would take over the park and appoint a committee to draw up the terms of a lease was carried by a large majority.

The club spent the not inconsiderable sum of £200 to prepare its new home, with the site being large enough for two excellent pitches. These ran in an east-west direction, but unfortunately, this would prove to be unsatisfactory because wind regularly affected play. Spectators stood behind a stout rope on raised banking and a pavilion, together with the unroofed wooden stand from across the road, stood on the Gorgie Road side of the field.

The new Tynecastle Park was a handsome credit to the club, although the Edinburgh Evening News, while delighted at the overall stadium, was forced to report, "the facilities for entering were very poor with the crushing and squeezing to

clear the barricade at times alarming. The entrance, which was along a lane opposite Newton Street, needs work and the press men also need accommodation. The pitch was much better being perfectly level. The old pitch had a decided slope which often proved successful for the team winning the toss".

However, the new stadium pleased the 5,500 supporters who attended the opening match against the well-known professional club, Bolton Wanderers, on Saturday, April 10th 1886. On that special day, the sun shone, the enthusiasm was intense, and Hearts defeated the famous English side by 4-1.

With a low shot, Tommy Jenkinson scored the first goal at the new Tynecastle Park, after only five minutes. Rab Henderson with two goals and Bobby McNeill raised the score to 4-0 before the Wanderers secured a late consolation. The ball went through the Hearts goal off a post, following a wild scramble involving about ten players. Accordingly, the scorer of the first opposition goal at Tynecastle was not identified. In the early days of football, a group of forwards often forced the ball over the line and this was referred to as a "scrimmage".

ASSOCIATION FOOTBALL FIXTURE.

OPENING OF NEW GROUND
At TYNECASTLE PARK, DALRY.
BOLTON WANDERERS V.
HEART OF MID-LOTHIAN.
On SATURDAY, 10th APRIL.
Kick off at 4 o'clock prompt. Admission, 6d. Ladies free.
Grand Stand, 6d extra. Cars from Register (every few
minutes) run close to Entrance Gate.
Members' Tickets not now available for Grand Stand.

Hearts' historic team was: Willie Gibson; Jimmy Adams and George Fairweather; Geordie Whyte, Davie Aitken and James Fraser; Tommy Jenkinson, Willie Mackay, Rab Henderson, Jimmy Common and Bobby McNeill.

WHAT'S IN THE HEARTS MUSEUM?

Join us as we explore our more unusual objects...

What kind of things would you EXPECT to see when you visit our Hearts Museum?

Footballs? Yes! Football Shirts? Of course! Trophies? We've got lots!

Did you know though, that when Hearts play teams from outside of Scotland, it's traditional for the teams to exchange gifts? The gifts usually reflect the Football Club, the city or even the country that they come from.

Our favourite gifts displayed in the museum all happen to be ANIMALS!

First is the Puffin... all the way from ICELAND!

When Hearts played IBV-Vestmannaeyjar in the UEFA Cup prelim round, they presented us with this stuffed puffin! There are estimated to be between 8 and 10 million puffins in Iceland. What makes them special is the penguin-like colour with a very colourful beak.

What do you think Hearts give other teams as gifts?

Traditionally we gave Edinburgh Crystal glasses in the olden days... these days we usually give a traditional Scottish Quaich, and if they're really lucky, a bottle of whisky thrown in!

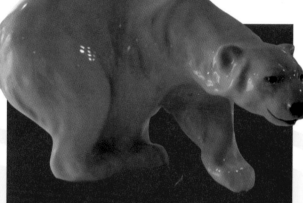

Next is our very own Liver Bird!

A gift from Liverpool, from 2012 in the Europa League Play-off

A Liver Bird is a mythical creature, which is the symbol of the English city of Liverpool. It is also seen on the crest of Liverpool FC.

And last but not least, is our Polar Bear

A gift from the Hearts 1913/14 tour to Denmark, this makes the Polar Bear the oldest animal in the museum at 108 years old!

Polar bears are not actually found within the borders of Denmark but rather in Greenland, which is a part of Danish territory. Did you know? The polar bear is actually classed as a vulnerable species because climate change is damaging their environment.

TOMMY WALKER

A LEADER OF MEN

By David Speed

GET TO KNOW HEARTS' GREATEST EVER MANAGER

During a lifetime of service to Hearts, Tommy Walker enhanced the reputation of the club worldwide. When he was manager, his teams were acclaimed for their skillful style and sporting approach. This perfectly mirrored the architect, a revered figure in Hearts' history and one of Scotland's greatest football ambassadors.

Born at Livingston Station in May 1915, Tommy left school at the age of fourteen and worked in a paper mill and then a shale oil works. In March 1932, he was taken onto Hearts' ground staff with the former Schoolboy Internationalist having gained juvenile experience with Livingston Violet and Broxburn Rangers. He then tasted junior football with Linlithgow Rose until May 1932 when, at the age of seventeen, he was able to sign a professional contract for Hearts.

Tommy Walker, second from left on the front row, with his all-conquering Hearts side.

MIDFIELD MAESTRO

Tommy's brilliant ball control and his wonderful passing and dribbling skills, quickly set him on the path to become Britain's finest playmaker. In fact, within months of his debut, Hearts had English clubs enquiring about his transfer. This continued throughout Tommy's career, to the dismay of Hearts' fans, who even held protest meetings when Arsenal looked set to secure his transfer in 1935 with a then astonishing offer of £12,000. All the Londoners could negotiate was first-refusal.

When only nineteen, Tommy earned the first of 20 consecutive International caps. His most famous appearance in dark blue undoubtedly came at Wembley in 1936 when he earned Scotland a 1-1 draw with a penalty kick, holding his nerve after the ball was repeatedly blown off the spot. Two years later he returned to Wembley to score the only goal in Scotland's victory, one of nine he netted for his country.

Tommy also earned five League International caps and represented Scotland eleven times in Wartime/Victory Internationals. In addition, he appeared ten times for the SFA on a tour of North America in 1935 and, in August that year, Tommy played in the Jubilee Trust Fund game against England. He would have been Hearts' most capped player, but for the Second World War.

He was modest, but the Scotsman in February 1936 noted, "whether going through on his own or sending out an inviting pass to a colleague, he was always a menace to his opponents. Added to that, the readiness and power of his shooting made him the complete footballer."

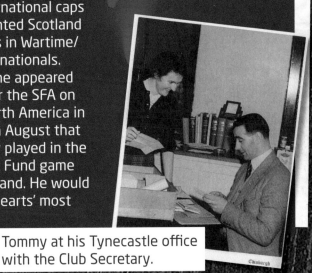

Tommy at his Tynecastle office with the Club Secretary.

SERVING HIS COUNTRY

Tommy assisted Hearts to second place in the League in 1937/38 and to the Cup Semi-finals in 1934/35. He was also the inspiration behind the club reaching the Wartime Cup Final in 1940/41 and to become runners-up in the East & North Division in 1939/40. Although he had no winners' medals to show for his efforts, there was a market for quality entertainment and Tommy Walker and his Hearts colleagues earned the highest accolades in this regard.

Hearts' star man received a Testimonial in April 1938 when 19,061 fans watched the maroons defeat Derby County by 2-1. Around this time Tommy expressed an intertest in joining the Ministry, but this ambition was frustrated in September 1939 by the outbreak of the Second World War. He enlisted in the Royal Signals Corps and Tommy was a Captain in the Welfare Division. During over five years of service, he spent long periods overseas. However, when at home, Hearts' idol always turned out in maroon and he was also a guest player with Chelsea and Bradford Park Avenue.

Tommy played many Army International and representative games, and while overseas, his touring team boosted morale among the troops. He was certainly a popular figure when Hearts visited Germany in June 1946 and Tommy scored two goals as the Combined Services were defeated by 3-2.

Having played for Chelsea during the War, Tommy was seen as the man to bring out the best in their young team. As a result, in September 1946, the Londoners paid £6,000 for his transfer.

HEARTS' IDEAL MANAGER

In December 1948, Tommy returned to Edinburgh as Assistant Manager/Secretary under Davie McLean. When he stopped playing, Tommy had scored a mighty 224 goals in 408 competitive matches for Hearts.

On Mr. McLean's untimely death in February 1951, Tommy took over the team affairs and fashioned brilliantly balanced squads that led Hearts through its finest era. In record breaking style, his team won the League Championship twice, the Scottish Cup once, and the Scottish League Cup four times. In addition, he led Hearts on several prestigious overseas tours and into Europe for the first time. Despite this success, he never took credit; he gave it.

Hearts' new Manager did face some early challenges. Although his team reached the Scottish Cup Semi-Finals twice (1951-/52 and 1952/53) and finished runners-up in the League in 1953-/54, the supporters were restless after more barren years and the huge success of local rivals, Hibernian. In fact, in January 1953, Tommy Walker had to deny rumours that he was going out of football.

Nevertheless, one-by-one, his plans came to fruition. This included a significant improvement in fitness after John Harvey was promoted to Trainer in May 1952. Tommy also rationalized the scouting staff and for several years, he took part in practice matches in order to closely assess his squad. Among Tommy's masterstrokes was handing key-roles to John Cumming and Davie Mackay. These two gave Hearts a formidable backbone and Hearts no longer folded after losing a goal.

SUCCESS AT LONG LAST

Overseas tours to Germany and Sweden increased the Manager's knowledge of his players and team spirit was greatly enhanced, particularly after the tour of South Africa in the summer of 1954. In October that year, Hearts beat Motherwell in the League Cup Final to bring major honours back to Tynecastle for the first time since 1906. This long-awaited breakthrough was the start of something really big.

Tommy Walker went on to fashion some dynamic squads that added three more successes in the League Cup in 1958/59, 1959/60 and 1962/63. Hearts also won the Scottish Cup Final in 1955/56 (3-1 against Celtic) and were League Champions in 1957/58 and 1959/60. The first League success was achieved in remarkable style with record goals scored (132) and points won (62 under the two points for a win system). He also led Hearts into Europe for the first time.

For generations, Hearts had been admired for the quality of their football and classy individual players. Walker had added key-men to the squad he inherited and produced winners through proper direction, quality training, sound recruitment and harnessing individual genius. This was not appreciated in the west, where most preferred Hearts to be good losers and not challenge the dominance of the Old Firm.

In 1958, Tommy Walker was suggested as a future Manager of Scotland and then in November 1960, he received an OBE from Her Majesty the Queen for his services to football. This was welcomed throughout the game and was a great honour to Tommy, his family, and the Heart of Midlothian Football Club. Despite all that he had achieved, he never took credit; he gave it.

In addition to the winning campaigns, Hearts were also runners-up in the League in 1953/54, 1956/57, 1958/59 and 1964/65. The team reached the League Cup Final in 1961/62, and the reserves successfully supported the senior side.

Tommy at his desk at Tynecastle.

Pre-match pitch inspection at a frozen Tynecastle.

CHANGING TIMES

Scottish football faced many challenges in the 1960s, with rising costs and falling attendances due to the range of leisure facilities now within reach of the public. Hearts also had to upgrade the ground, with floodlights and covered accommodation, and the sale of Mackay, Thomson and Young was necessary to balance the budget. In addition, in 1961, the Football League abolished its £20 per week maximum wage and the drain of quality players to England gathered pace. Clubs now had to survive on fund-raising groups to make up for missing spectators.

Players who remained demanded more money and Tommy had to rebuild under strained circumstances. Although it was not his preferred method, he entered the transfer market, but it was impossible to recruit the same quality as

the club had possessed in the fifties. Tommy also had to deal with social changes and disciplinary issues that he had never previously encountered.
In addition, tactics had moved away from five forwards and Scotland started to see an influx of Scandinavian players.

Tommy Walker faced up to the challenges with fortitude, but when Hearts lost the League Championship on the final day of the 1964/65 season, this proved to be a watershed for the Manager. Hearts fell to seventh in the League in 1965/66 and to address the decline, it was agreed to appoint a full-time Secretary, because office work had become onerous. The manager required more time with the players and Tommy recommended that John Harvey take overall control of training and scouting, with Donald

McLeod as Trainer and John Cumming his assistant.

Nevertheless, the directors felt that an irreparable breach had grown between the manager and the dressing room, and because they intended to invoke the six-month option clause in his contract, Tommy Walker resigned on October 3rd 1966.

Although he held positions with Dunfermline Athletic and Raith Rovers, his heart lay at Tynecastle Park. In a very popular move, Tommy returned as a Director in October 1974 and served on the board until his retirement in 1980. Tommy Walker was a real star, with infinite talent and class, both on and off the field. His contribution to the fame and reputation of the Hearts is unsurpassed and it was indeed a sad day when he passed away in January 1993 at St. Columba's Hospice.

WE'VE GOT OUR TYNECASTLE BACK

On Sunday 21st August, Tynecastle Park returned to capacity for the first time since March 2020 as 17,449 fans packed in to see the Jambos play out a 1-1 draw with Aberdeen.

Photo: David Mollison

John Souttar celebrates scoring the winner against Celtic on July 31st 2021 in front of 5000+ fans at Tynecastle. The outpouring of emotion was tangible as the Jambos played out a home league fixture in front of fans for the first time since March 2020.

Photo: David Mollison

KITTED OUT

The question for me is why is the Asics Inter Milan style kit so popular amongst fans, and why the groundswell of support to bring back an updated version? Let me provide a few really interesting points about the away shirt from 1993/94. It was only worn four times by the first team squad.

In non-competitive games we wore it against Everton on the 2nd of August 1993 in Henry Smith's Testimonial. We wore it again against Middlesbrough in a preseason friendly at the start of season 1994/95 on the 6th of August.

As far as I am aware, we only ever wore it twice in competitive matches and on both occasions, this was against today's opposition

Aberdeen, both times at Pittodrie. In fact, we are undefeated in competitive matches wearing the shirt with Hearts drawing 0-0 on the 5th of October 1993 and then coming away with a 1-0 win thanks to a Scott Leitch goal in the 31st minute on the 5th of March 1994.

I find it very curious that a shirt only seen in public four times has become so popular amongst the Hearts support. I liken it to the film *Shawshank Redemption* which on release was coolly received but today has been watched by millions and is considered a classic.

The shirt itself was manufactured by Asics who would provide shirts for seasons 1993/1994 and 1994/95. It had a black collar with two large white buttons. The body of the shirt had large vertical black and aqua stripes. The long sleeve version has black cuffs that match the collar. The sponsor would remain as Strongbow. The sponsor logo was heat pressed flock and would appear centrally on the shirt.

There are subtle differences between a replica shirt and a match shirt. The replica has a heat pressed club plastic badge and embroidered logo. The long sleeve version was not made available to the general public. A player's shirt has both an embroidered logo and club badge.

The shirt pictured was worn by Gary Locke during the 5th of March game, coming on as a substitute in the 84th minute for Wayne Foster.

Gary is a lifelong Hearts supporter and a firm favourite with the support. He made 189 appearances for Hearts, pitching in with 6 goals. The lure of English football was too much for Gary as he left Hearts for Bradford City to join his old gaffer Jim Jeffries in January 2001.

He would return to Hearts as a coach in February 2010 and would be part of the coaching staff that won the Scottish Cup against Hibernian in 2012.

Locke was placed in caretaker charge of the team after the departure of John McGlynn in February 2013. He was subsequently appointed on a permanent basis, on a contract until the end of the 2013/14 season. Gary was welcomed back to the club on a full-time basis as the Club's Principal Ambassador in July 2017.

Grant Young is a Hearts shirt collector and is currently writing a book. He can be contacted at **jambojim190512@yahoo.com** or via twitter **@heartsshirts**

THE
21/22
LOOK

HEARTS
HEARTS
HEARTS
HEARTS

HOME

WE   ARE   HEARTS
WE   ARE   HEARTS
RE   HEARTS
RE   HEARTS
RE   HEARTS

THIRD

GK

AWAY

The Umbro kits for the 21/22 season
all available from heartsdirect.co.uk!

ANSWERS

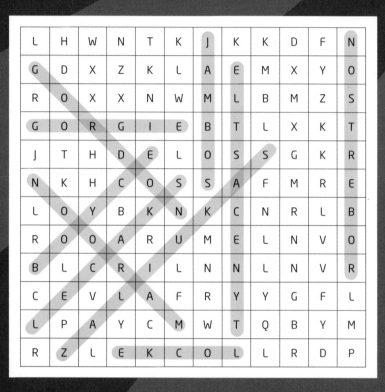

L	H	W	N	T	K	J	K	K	D	F	N
G	D	X	Z	K	L	A	E	M	X	Y	O
R	O	X	X	N	W	M	L	B	M	Z	S
G	O	R	G	I	E	B	T	L	X	K	T
J	T	H	D	E	L	O	S	S	G	K	R
N	K	H	C	O	S	S	A	F	M	R	E
L	O	Y	B	K	N	K	C	N	R	L	B
R	O	O	A	R	U	M	E	L	N	V	O
B	L	C	R	I	L	N	N	L	N	V	R
C	E	V	L	A	F	R	Y	Y	G	F	L
L	P	A	Y	C	M	W	T	Q	B	Y	M
R	Z	L	E	K	C	O	L	L	R	D	P

WHO AM I?

Paul Hartley

SPOT THE BALL

FORMER PLAYER QUIZ

1. David Milinkovic
2. Andy Webster
3. Mark de Vries
4. Gary Mackay
5. Rudi Skacel

6. David Weir
7. Craig Levein
8. Takis Fyssas
9. Graeme Weir
10. Kyle Lafferty